KNOW YOUR GOVERNMENT

The Internal Revenue Service

KNOW YOUR GOVERNMENT

The Internal Revenue Service

Jack Taylor

CHELSEA HOUSE PUBLISHERS
NEW YORK • NEW HAVEN • PHILADELPHIA

Copyright © 1987 by Chelsea House Publishers, 5014 West Chester Pike, Edgemont, Pa. 19028. All rights reserved.
Reproduction in whole or part by any means whatsoever without permission of the publisher is prohibited by law.
Printed in the United States of America.

KG2-012086

Library of Congress Cataloging-in-Publication Data

Taylor, Jack, 1935-
   Internal Revenue Service.
   (Know your government)
   Bibliography: p. 89
   Includes index.
   1. United States. Internal Revenue Service—History.
2. Tax administration and procedure—United States—History.
I. Title. II. Series: Know your government (New York, N.Y.)
HJ5018.T36   1987   353.0072'4   86-20803

ISBN 0-87754-823-4

General Editor: Professor Fred L. Israel
Project Editor: Nancy Priff
Art Director: Maureen McCafferty
Series Designer: Anita Noble
Chief Copy Editor: Melissa R. Padovani
Project Coordinator: Kathleen P. Luczak

ABOUT THE COVER

To many people, the Internal Revenue Service—the nation's tax collector—is just a faceless mass of forms and reports. And every year, thousands of individuals rush to beat the midnight, April 15th, deadline for mailing their tax forms to the IRS.

CONTENTS

Introduction 7
1 The Nation's Tax Collector 17
2 Why Americans Pay Taxes 21
3 A History of the IRS 29
4 The IRS Organization 49
5 How the IRS Works 63
6 The IRS of the Future 85
Glossary 88
Selected References 89
Index..90

KNOW YOUR GOVERNMENT

Other titles in this series include:

The American Red Cross
The Bureau of Indian Affairs
The Center for Disease Control
The Central Intelligence Agency
The Children, Youth, and
 Families Division
The Department of Agriculture
The Department of the Air Force
The Department of the Army
The Department of Commerce
The Department of Defense
The Department of Education
The Department of Energy
The Department of Health
 and Human Services
The Department of Housing
 and Urban Development
The Department of the Interior
The Department of Justice
The Department of Labor
The Department of the Navy
The Department of State
The Department of
 Transportation
The Department of the Treasury
The Drug Enforcement Agency
The Environmental
 Protection Agency
The Equal Opportunities
 Commission
The Federal Aviation
 Administration
The Federal Bureau of
 Investigation
The Federal Communications
 Commission
The Federal Elections
 Commission
The Federal Railroad
 Administration
The Food and Drug
 Administration
The Food and Nutrition Division
The House of Representatives
The Immigration and
 Naturalization Service
The Internal Revenue Service
The Interstate Commerce
 Commission
The National Foundation on the
 Arts and Humanities
The National Park Service
The National Science Foundation
The Presidency
The Securities and
 Exchange Commission
The Selective Service System
The Senate
The Small Business
 Administration
The Smithsonian
The Supreme Court
The Tennessee Valley Authority
The U.S. Information Agency
The U.S. Arms Control and
 Disarmament Agency
The U.S. Coast Guard
The U.S. Commission on
 Civil Rights
The U.S. Fish and Wildlife Service
The U.S. Mint
The U.S. Nuclear Regulatory
 Commission
The U.S. Postal Service
The U.S. Secret Service
The Veteran's Administration

INTRODUCTION

Government: Crises of Confidence

Arthur M. Schlesinger, jr.

From the start, Americans have regarded their government with a mixture of reliance and mistrust. The men who founded the republic did not doubt the indispensability of government. "If men were angels," observed the 51st Federalist Paper, "no government would be necessary." But men are not angels. Since human beings are subject to wicked as well as to noble impulses, government was deemed essential to assure freedom and order.

At the same time, the American revolutionaries knew that government could also become a source of injury and oppression. The men who gathered in Philadelphia in 1787 to write the Constitution therefore had two purposes in mind. They wanted to establish a strong central authority and to limit that central authority's capacity to abuse its power.

To prevent the abuse of power, the founding fathers wrote two basic principles into the new Constitution. The principle of federalism divided power between the state governments and the central authority. The principle of the separation of powers subdivided the central authority itself into three branches—the executive, the legislative, and the judiciary—so that "each may be a check on the other." The *Know Your Government* series focuses on the major executive departments and agencies in these branches of the federal government.

The Constitution did not plan the executive branch in any detail. After vesting the executive power in the president, it assumed the existence of "executive departments" without specifying what these departments should be. Congress began defining their functions in 1789 by creating the Departments of State, Treasury, and War. The secretaries in charge of these departments made up President Washington's first cabinet. Congress also provided for a legal officer, and President Washington soon invited the attorney general, as he was called, to attend cabinet meetings. As need required, Congress created more executive departments.

Setting up the cabinet was only the first step in organizing the American state. With almost no guidance from the Constitution, President Washington, seconded by Alexander Hamilton, his brilliant secretary of the treasury, equipped the infant republic with a working administrative structure. The Federalists believed in both executive energy and executive accountability and set high standards for public appointments. The Jeffersonian opposition had less faith in strong government and preferred local government to the central authority. But when Jefferson himself became president in 1801, although he set out to change the direction of policy, he found no reason to alter the framework the Federalists had erected.

By 1801 there were about 3,000 federal civilian employees in a nation of a little more than 5 million people. Growth in territory and population steadily enlarged national responsibilities. Thirty years later, when Jackson was president, there were more than 11,000 government workers in a nation of 13 million.

The federal establishment was increasing at a faster rate than the population.

Jackson's presidency brought significant changes in the federal service. He believed that the executive branch contained too many officials who saw their jobs as "species of property" and as "a means of promoting individual interest." Against the idea of a permanent service based on life tenure, Jackson argued for the periodic redistribution of federal offices, contending that this was the democratic way and that official duties could be made "so plain and simple that men of intelligence may readily qualify themselves for their performance." He called this policy rotation-in-office. His opponents called it the spoils system.

In fact, partisan legend exaggerated the extent of Jackson's removals. More than 80 percent of federal officeholders retained their jobs. Jackson discharged no larger a proportion of government workers than Jefferson had done a generation earlier. But the rise in these years of mass political parties gave federal patronage new importance as a means of building the party and of rewarding activists. Jackson's successors were less restrained in the distribution of spoils. As the federal establishment grew—to nearly 40,000 by 1861—the politicization of the public service excited increasing concern.

After the Civil War the spoils system became a major political issue. High-minded men condemned it as the root of all political evil. The spoilsmen, said the British commentator James Bryce, "have distorted and depraved the mechanism of politics." Patronage, by giving jobs to unqualified, incompetent, and dishonest persons, lowered the standards of public service and nourished corrupt political machines. Office-seekers pursued presidents and cabinet secretaries without mercy. "Patronage," said Ulysses S. Grant after his presidency, "is the bane of the presidential office." "Every time I appoint someone to office," said another political leader, "I make a hundred enemies and one ingrate." George William Curtis, the president of the National Civil Service Reform League, summed up the indictment. He said,

> The theory which perverts public trusts into party spoils, making public employment dependent upon personal favor and not on proved merit, necessarily ruins the self-respect of public employees, destroys the function of party in a republic, prostitutes elections into a desperate strife for personal profit, and degrades the national character by lowering the moral tone and standard of the country.

The object of civil service reform was to promote efficiency and honesty in the public service and to bring about the ethical regeneration of public life. Over bitter opposition from politicians, the reformers in 1883 passed the Pendleton Act, establishing a bipartisan Civil Service Commission, competitive examinations, and appointment on merit. The Pendleton Act also gave the president authority to extend by executive order the number of "classified" jobs—that is, jobs subject to the merit system. The act applied initially only to about 14,000 of the more than 100,000 federal positions. But by the end of the 19th century 40 percent of federal jobs had moved into the classified category.

Civil service reform was in part a response to the growing complexity of American life. As society grew more organized and problems more technical, official duties were no longer so plain and simple that any person of intelligence could perform them. In public service, as in other areas, the all-round man was yielding ground to the expert, the amateur to the professional. The excesses of the spoils system thus provoked the counter-ideal of scientific public administration, separate from politics and, as far as possible, insulated against it.

The cult of the expert, however, had its own excesses. The idea that administration could be divorced from policy was an illusion. And in the realm of policy, the expert, however much segregated from partisan politics, can never attain perfect objectivity. He remains the prisoner of his own set of values. It is these values rather than technical expertise that determine fundamental judgments of public policy. To turn over such judgments to experts, moreover, would be to abandon democracy itself; for in a democracy final decisions must be made by the people and their elected representatives. "The business of the expert," the British political scientist Harold Laski rightly said, "is to be on tap and not on top."

Politics, however, were deeply ingrained in American folkways. This meant intermittent tension between the presidential government, elected every four years by the people, and the permanent government, which saw presidents come and go while it went on forever. Sometimes the permanent government knew better than its political masters; sometimes it opposed or sabotaged valuable new initiatives. In the end a strong president with effective cabinet secretaries could make the permanent government responsive to presidential purpose, but it was often an exasperating struggle.

The struggle within the executive branch was less important, however, than the growing impatience with bureaucracy in society as a whole. The 20th century saw a considerable expansion of the federal establishment. The Great Depression and the New Deal led the national government to take on a variety of new responsibilities. The New Deal extended the federal regulatory apparatus. By 1940, in a nation of 130 million people, the number of federal workers for the first time passed the 1 million mark. The Second World War brought federal civilian employment to 3.8 million in 1945. With peace, the federal establishment declined to around 2 million by 1950. Then growth resumed, reaching 2.8 million by the 1980s.

The New Deal years saw rising criticism of "big government" and "bureaucracy." Businessmen resented federal regulation. Conservatives worried about the impact of paternalistic government on individual self-reliance, on community responsibility, and on economic and personal freedom. The nation in effect renewed the old debate between Hamilton and Jefferson in the early republic, although with an ironic exchange of positions. For the Hamiltonian constituency, the "rich and well-born," once the advocate of affirmative government, now condemned government intervention, while the Jeffersonian constituency, the plain people, once the advocate of a weak central government and of states' rights, now favored government intervention.

In the 1980s, with the presidency of Ronald Reagan, the debate has burst out with unusual intensity. According to conservatives, government intervention abridges liberty, stifles enterprise, and is inefficient, wasteful, and arbitrary. It disturbs the harmony of the self-adjusting market and creates worse troubles than it solves. Get government off our backs, according to the popular cliché, and our problems will solve themselves. When government is necessary, let it be at the local level, close to the people. Above all, stop the inexorable growth of the federal government.

In fact, for all the talk about the "swollen" and "bloated" bureaucracy, the federal establishment has not been growing as inexorably as many Americans seem to believe. In 1949, it consisted of 2.1 million people. Thirty years later, while the country had grown by 70 million, the federal force had grown only by 750,000. Federal workers were a smaller percentage of the population in 1985 than they were in 1955—or in 1940. The federal establishment, in short, has not kept pace with population growth. Moreover, national defense and the postal service account for 60 percent of federal employment.

Why then the widespread idea about the remorseless growth of government? It is partly because in the 1960s the national government assumed new and intrusive functions:

affirmative action in civil rights, environmental protection, safety and health in the workplace, community organization, legal aid to the poor. Although this enlargement of the federal regulatory role was accompanied by marked growth in the size of government on all levels, the expansion has taken place primarily in state and local government. Whereas the federal force increased by only 27 percent in the 30 years after 1950, the state and local government force increased by an astonishing 212 percent.

Despite the statistics, the conviction flourishes in some minds that the national government is a steadily growing behemoth swallowing up the liberties of the people. The foes of Washington prefer local government, feeling it is closer to the people and therefore allegedly more responsive to popular needs. Obviously there is a great deal to be said for settling local questions locally. But local government is characteristically the government of the locally powerful. Historically, the way the locally powerless have won their human and constitutional rights has often been through appeal to the national government. The national government has vindicated racial justice against local bigotry, defended the Bill of Rights against local vigilantism, and protected natural resources against local greed. It has civilized industry and secured the rights of labor organizations. Had the states' rights creed prevailed, there would perhaps still be slavery in the United States.

The national authority, far from diminishing the individual, has given most Americans more personal dignity and liberty than ever before. The individual freedoms destroyed by the increase in national authority have been in the main the freedom to deny black Americans their rights as citizens; the freedom to put small children to work in mills and immigrants in sweatshops; the freedom to pay starvation wages, require barbarous working hours, and permit squalid working conditions; the freedom to deceive in the sale of goods and securities; the freedom to pollute the environment—all freedoms that, one supposes, a civilized nation can readily do without.

"Statements are made," said President John F. Kennedy in 1963, "labelling the Federal Government an outsider, an intruder, an adversary. ... The United States Government is not a stranger or not an enemy. It is the people of fifty states joining in a national effort. ... Only a great national effort by a great people working together can explore the mysteries of space, harvest the products at the bottom of the ocean, and mobilize the human, natural, and material resources of our lands."

So an old debate continues. However, Americans are of two minds. When pollsters ask large, spacious questions—Do you think government has become too involved in your lives? Do you think government should stop regulating business?—a sizable majority opposes big government. But when asked specific questions about the practical work of government—Do you favor social security? unemployment compensation? Medicare? health and safety standards in factories? environmental protection? government guarantee of jobs for everyone seeking employment? price and wage controls when inflation threatens?—a sizable majority approves of intervention.

In general, Americans do not want less government. What they want is more efficient government. They want government to do a better job. For a time in the 1970s, with Vietnam and Watergate, Americans lost confidence in the national government. In 1964, more than three-quarters of those polled had thought the national government could be trusted to do right most of the time. By 1980 only one-quarter was prepared to offer such trust. But by 1984 trust in the federal government to manage national affairs had climbed back to 45 percent.

Bureaucracy is a term of abuse. But it is impossible to run any large organization, whether public or private, without a bureaucracy's division of labor and hierarchy of authority. And we live in a world of large organizations. Without bureaucracy modern society would collapse. The problem is not to abolish bureaucracy, but to make it flexible, efficient, and capable of innovation.

Two hundred years after the drafting of the Constitution, Americans still regard government with a mixture of reliance and mistrust—a good combination. Mistrust is the best way to keep government reliable. Informed criticism is the means of correcting governmental inefficiency, incompetence, and arbitrariness; that is, of best enabling government to play its essential role. For without government, we cannot attain the goals of the founding fathers. Without an understanding of government, we cannot have the informed criticism that makes government do the job right. It is the duty of every American citizen to *Know Your Government*—which is what this series is all about.

As the nation's tax collector, the IRS gathers and processes income information from individuals and businesses.

ONE

The Nation's Tax Collector

Sometimes when people discuss the Internal Revenue Service (IRS), they speak in hushed tones. A hint of awe or fear may even creep into their voices. Why does a government agency evoke such a response? Probably because the IRS has a great deal of power and because its activities touch nearly everyone in the United States.

The goal of the IRS, America's tax collecting agency, is to get every taxpayer to comply voluntarily with the tax laws. To achieve this goal, the agency advises taxpayers of their rights and responsibilities, communicates legal requirements to them, helps them comply with the tax laws, and impartially enforces the tax laws when necessary.

The IRS is one of the first federal agencies that most people deal with personally. As soon as a person gets his first job, he must communicate with the IRS by completing a W-4 form. If the new employee expects to earn more than a minimum income, this form tells the IRS how much tax money to withhold from each paycheck. If the new employee expects to earn less than the minimum, this form can be used to request an exemption from withholding tax. So the IRS and the taxes it collects ultimately affect everyone.

The IRS's basic responsibilities include resolving taxpayers' complaints; educating and serving the taxpayers; developing, assessing, and collecting internal revenue taxes; and preparing and issuing new tax rules and regulations. Because the IRS collects most of the tax money that runs the federal government, it keeps records on almost every American citizen and questions millions of families and businesses each year about their finances. If an individual doesn't pay his taxes, the IRS has the power to place a lien (hold) on his property and wages until the tax debt is satisfied. If necessary, the IRS, with the courts' help, can force an individual to sell his property to pay his taxes. Although the IRS doesn't use its special collection power very often, it can take suspected tax evaders to court and even send them to jail if they're convicted.

Despite this great power, the IRS deals routinely with most of the millions of citizens paying taxes each year, and although

For most, a W-4 form is the first contact with the IRS.

it handles huge sums of money, it has had very few serious scandals in its history. In 1984 it collected and accounted for $680 billion, and every year it's responsible for similar amounts of money. Not only is the IRS an efficient tax collector, but it's also the most economical tax collector in the world—it costs less than 50 cents to collect each $100 of taxes.

Part of the reason for the IRS's efficiency is that the tax system itself is voluntary—Americans assess taxes on themselves instead of having tax collectors assess them. This voluntary tax system makes it inexpensive for the government to enforce. Another reason for its low cost is that taxpayers and businessmen collect much of the tax money for the government and absorb some of the collection costs.

In recent years, the IRS has been confronted with a number of problems including increasingly complex tax laws, internal organizational problems, a rise in the number of taxpayers and tax records, an increase in the number of dissatisfied taxpayers, and a tarnished public image. Public dissatisfaction with taxes seems to be leading to changes in the tax system that could help the IRS solve its problems.

Like most other problems in the government, tax questions will remain for the next generation of citizens to try to solve. So today's young people can not only expect to pay taxes, but also to help decide what kind of taxes we should have and how they should be collected.

Before the American Revolution, colonists sometimes tarred and feathered the excise men sent by the king to collect tax money required by the Stamp Act.

TWO

Why Americans Pay Taxes

Taxes have always been a sensitive subject with Americans. Even before America was a country, its colonists started a revolution at least in part because they didn't like the way they were being taxed. At the Boston Tea Party, they threw tea overboard rather than pay tax on it. Throughout the nation's history, Americans have argued and sometimes fought over taxation. Some of that feeling persists today—practically everyone believes that he pays too much tax and that others pay too little.

But if Americans are a democratic people who govern themselves and who dislike taxes, why do they have them? Why don't they elect leaders who will do away with taxes altogether? Because the nation has to have an income to cover its expenses. It can't rely on contributions, because some people wouldn't pay their fair share. And it can't borrow the money, because no one would lend money to a government that had no income. So the nation must have taxes.

This commonsense approach is one way to explain why taxes exist. But another approach is this: taxes are the price people pay for government. For example, the government manages transportation, including roads. Because the government needs money to provide this service, it collects a tax on each gallon of gasoline that motorists use. So part of the price of gas goes to the oil company to pay for the fuel, and part of it—the tax part—goes to the government to pay for the roads.

Tax money also finances national defense. Americans have always been willing to pay to protect their country from foreign enemies, and they have agreed to raise taxes in times of war. The federal government first raised taxes to pay off revolutionary war debts. Since then, almost every war involving the United States has caused an increase in taxes.

The government taxes gasoline to help pay for the roads.

Taxes pay for defense projects, such as the launching of military communications satellites.

Kinds of Taxes

Even when a citizen realizes that the nation needs some taxes, he may not necessarily like the type or amount of taxes he must pay. The American colonists went to war with England because they objected to the kinds of taxes England imposed on them, and because they objected to their lack of representation in deciding how they would be taxed. They believed that taxation without representation was tyranny.

Today critics may complain about high taxes or prefer the use of different kinds of taxes, but they can't say that they're taxed without fair representation. Americans elect congressional representatives who pass the nation's tax laws. These elected officials also pay a great deal of attention to the public's reaction, and very unpopular taxes do not last long. So the government needs the consent of many of the people for taxation.

But no tax receives unanimous consent. Three basic kinds of taxes exist, and each has its own distinct advantages and disadvantages.

The simplest tax is a head, or poll, tax. It's figured by counting citizens' heads and ordering each person to pay the government a certain amount of money every year. Most people think this type of tax is unfair, because everyone pays the same amount no matter how rich or poor he is. In addition, it's a difficult tax to collect, because some people have no money at all. For these reasons, no modern government depends on head taxes.

Another kind of tax is the taxation of the sale of goods. Collecting taxes is much easier if the money is available for collection. One way to ensure this is to collect the tax when money changes hands. That's why taxes on the sale of goods are popular with governments; if people are buying goods, they must have money. These taxes come in three forms: sales taxes, which are added on top of the purchase price of items; excise taxes, which are included in the price of certain goods, such as gasoline and cigarettes; and import taxes, or customs duties,

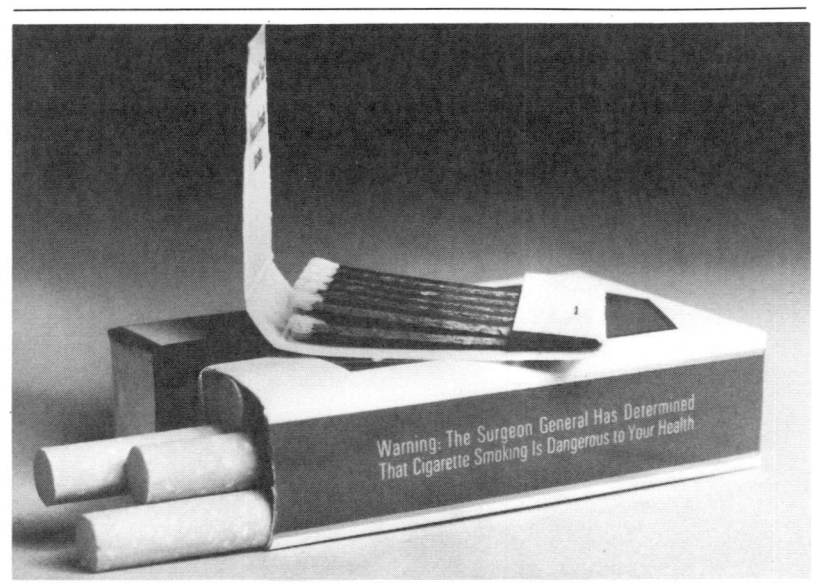

The price of a pack of cigarettes includes an excise tax.

which are added to the cost of foreign goods coming into the country.

Although taxes on goods are easy to collect and probably could supply enough money to run the government, these taxes present some major problems. For example, compared with the rich, the poor must spend a higher percentage of their money on living expenses, so a tax on spending means taxing the poor on more of their total income than the rich. Most people believe that those who can afford to pay more taxes ought to pay more, or at least that those who have money for luxuries ought to pay more than those who spend all of their money for necessities. Another problem is that taxes on goods increase their prices. For instance, a tax on gasoline makes it cost more at the gas pump. In some cases, that's exactly what the government wants to do. The government taxes some things, such as tobacco and alcohol, purposely to increase their cost and discourage their use. In general, however, most Americans think that the government should not interfere with prices for goods, because artificial pricing can upset the economy.

The third kind of tax is an income tax. Obviously, a good time to collect a tax is when people spend their money. But an even better time to collect a tax is when they receive payments. Typically, taxing money when it comes in—through income tax—is much easier than taxing money when it goes out. An example of this is our country's wage tax, which pays for social security.

So the best kind of tax is one that most people don't dislike too much, is relatively easy to collect, taxes people according to what they can afford, and doesn't upset the economy. For a long time, most Americans believed that the income tax met these criteria best. Since World War I, the income tax has been the federal government's main source of revenue. Although it isn't as popular now, the income tax is still believed to be the fairest tax.

This relief carving shows Roman soldiers paying a tax for settling in the Rhine. Many taxes in ancient Rome, including this one, required forceful collection.

Tax Collection

Governments collect different kinds of taxes in different ways. For example, head taxes, property taxes, and other taxes that required forceful collection from citizens were common during the Roman Empire. Taxes were collected on commission, and tax collectors often became very rich because they kept a part of everything they collected.

Taxes that were collected by watching the flow of money and goods, such as import taxes, needed a different kind of tax collector—one who could use accounting skills at some point in a business transaction. For years, the United States got most of its money from import taxes, and it still receives money from many of them today. These taxes bring in *external* revenue (money from outside of the country) and are collected by the Customs Bureau.

Later, excise and income taxes—collected inside the country—became important. These required different collection methods, so the government set up a new agency and called it the Bureau of *Internal* Revenue to distinguish it from the Customs Bureau. At first, the main sources of internal revenue were excise taxes on alcohol and tobacco. To collect taxes on these items, the IRS hired agents known as revenuers, to seek out goods that people had tried to avoid paying the tax for. These agents were often shown breaking up stills in cartoons and comic movies. Currently, the main source of internal revenue is the income tax—a complex tax that requires a great deal of information processing—so the IRS uses computer programmers and accountants to collect and track the tax.

IRS agents called revenuers broke up hidden stills used to make alcohol without paying tax on it.

The government needed to raise taxes to pay for cannons and other armaments bought for the Civil War.

THREE

A History of the IRS

By 1861, low taxes had become an established American tradition. Because taxes had been a major cause of the American Revolution, the new government had been very cautious about taxing its citizens. Under its first constitution, the Articles of Confederation, adopted in 1781, the federal government had no power of taxation; instead, state contributions were supposed to support the government.

The second constitution, the Constitution of 1789, gave the federal government the right to tax, but political fights over taxes continued. In 1792, a federal tax on whiskey was so unpopular that Pennsylvania farmers, who made whiskey from the corn they grew, beat up the tax collectors and threatened to hang them. President George Washington had to send troops to crush this revolt, which came to be called the Whiskey Rebellion.

Thomas Jefferson campaigned against the tax on whiskey and other internal taxes in 1800. When he won the presidency,

Washington sent troops to put down the Whiskey Rebellion.

all of these taxes were repealed. The government revived internal taxes on property and sales from 1812 to 1817 to pay for the War of 1812. But otherwise, between 1800 and 1861 the country had no internal revenue taxes at all. Because federal spending was low, money from import taxes and government land sales could finance all of it.

During these years, the system worked very well. In fact, in 1826 a congressional committee complained that the federal government had more money than it could spend. And by 1835 the entire national debt was paid off.

Money to Save the Union

The Civil War ended the government's ability to live on import taxes and land sales. By the time the war was over, America had federal excise taxes, income taxes, and a commissioner of internal revenue, all of which remain today.

In April of 1861, the state army of South Carolina attacked the United States Army at Fort Sumter in Charleston harbor. In response, President Abraham Lincoln called for 75,000 volunteers to join the United States Army to put down the rebellion. Obviously he expected a short war, because he asked the volunteers to serve for only three months.

Lincoln soon realized that his army couldn't suppress the rebellion in three months. By July of 1861, the Confederates had captured Fort Sumter, created their own government, and repelled Union forces at the Battle of Bull Run—the first of many battles. As Lincoln and the Congress started to prepare for a longer war, they considered how to pay for the soldiers, guns, ships, and other needed equipment. Because the federal government's only sources of income were import taxes and taxes on public land sales, the government leaders realized that they would need new taxes to finance the war.

The Civil War Revenue Act of August 5, 1861, taxed alcohol, tobacco, and hundreds of other products. It also introduced

The bombs that fell on Fort Sumter not only started the Civil War but also gave rise to the country's first income tax.

the country's first income tax. Because the government needed more money immediately, it passed another tax law, the Revenue Act of July 1, 1862, which increased the existing taxes and added more excise taxes and fees.

This dramatic increase in taxes demanded a new method of tax collection. So the Revenue Act of 1862 also established the office of commissioner of internal revenue in the Treasury Department and divided the country into 185 collection districts, each with its own assessor, who determined the amount of tax to be paid, and collector. This act also gave the commissioner the responsibility for collecting all of the country's internal taxes and the authority to enforce the law through prosecution and seizure, if necessary.

The job of commissioner of internal revenue promised to be difficult. The federal government hadn't collected excise taxes for more than 40 years, and no one in the country had ever collected income taxes. The nation was entrenched in a war and

A cartoon in 1862 expressed Lincoln's need for more money to pay for war expenses.

Boutwell set up the Bureau of Internal Revenue in eight months.

needed money as soon as it could be collected. And internal revenue workers and equipment were hard to get because the war effort required almost all available men and machines.

To fill this challenging position, President Lincoln appointed a Massachusetts lawyer, George S. Boutwell, as the first commissioner of internal revenue. Starting in July 1862 with only one clerk to help him, Boutwell developed a new government agency, the Bureau of Internal Revenue. This amazing man hired accounting clerks and tax collectors, wrote explanations of the new laws, designed tax forms, set up accounting procedures to record the money collected, organized a tax collecting force of almost 4,000 people, and retired to run for Congress, all in less than 8 months.

The new agency had to collect taxes on almost everything: deeds and other legal papers; sales of practically all products, including gunpowder, yachts, patent medicines, telegrams, playing cards, and feathers; and income from almost all sources. It also collected license fees from most trades and professions, such as carpenters, printers, and lawyers.

The way the Bureau of Internal Revenue collected these taxes was quite different from the way they're collected today. When the bureau began, the taxpayer listed his taxable sales or income on a form as we do now, but then the tax collector calculated the tax and told him how much he owed. For the income tax on workers, the tax collector told the employer how much an employee owed for the previous year's taxes. Then the employer withheld the taxes from the employee's wages or salary. Other people paid taxes at the local tax collector's office or at home when the tax collector came to get the money. Like the ancient Roman system, private contractors collected a lot of the taxes on commission, keeping a share of what they brought in.

In those days, people didn't seem so concerned about privacy. The tax collectors not only told employers how much tax each employee owed, but they also published everyone's income and tax payments in the newspapers. They felt this encouraged people to be honest about their incomes. If a taxpayer lied, his supervisor, neighbor, or other acquaintances might see the information and report him to the tax collectors.

The Fight Over Income Tax

The internal revenue system begun during the Civil War was so successful that the federal government has kept some kind of internal taxes ever since. However, the government dropped the most successful of these taxes—the income tax—shortly after the war ended.

The income tax caused controversy and major political conflicts for the rest of the 19th century. Because the income tax only affected people with very large incomes, wealthy people disliked it. To them, it was an unfair tax imposed on the upper classes by the lower classes. In contrast, people with small incomes liked the tax because they felt it made up for other taxes that took a bigger chunk of their incomes. A political struggle ensued. The low-income people outnumbered those with high incomes, so they had more votes and more power at the polls. But the rich—although fewer in number—had much more political influence.

First one side and then the other won the fight. In 1872, the upper class gained the advantage when the government repealed the income tax used to finance the Civil War. When Congress enacted a new income tax law in 1894, the lower class won the advantage, but lost it the following year, when the Supreme Court ruled the new tax law unconstitutional in the *Pollack v. Farmer's Loan and Trust Company* case. The lower class fought back to gain the upper hand in this political struggle. In 1913, the states ratified the Constitution's Sixteenth Amendment, giving Congress the power to "tax all incomes, from whatever source derived," and Congress passed another income tax law. Ever since then, the income tax has been a part of American life.

During this conflict over income tax, the Bureau of Internal Revenue continued to collect excise and other taxes. For most of the period, taxes on whiskey and tobacco products were the

In 1895, the income tax law was declared unconstitutional, and cartoons reflected its unpopularity.

WITHOUT A FRIEND.

To prepare for World War I, the United States began to arm its ships and raise taxes to finance its activities.

main source of internal revenue for the federal government. The Spanish-American War (1898-1899) required financing, as wars usually do, so the government doubled the taxes on beer and tobacco and put excise taxes on several new products, including chewing gum. The Spanish-American War was small and didn't require large amounts of revenue to finance it. However, the *next* war was different.

World War I

For the generation that lived through it, the first world war was known as the Great War or simply the World War. The next generation renamed it World War I because it got involved in a second world war. But no matter what it was called, the first world war was certainly very expensive.

By 1916, Germany and Austria had been fighting England, France, and Russia for two years. The war was beginning to spill over into other countries. The United States started arming its ships and taking other steps to prepare for war, such as raising taxes. By the time America actually entered the war in 1917, the Bureau of Internal Revenue was already collecting the new taxes. The War Revenue Act of 1917 allowed it to collect taxes on income, beverages, tobacco, excess profits, public utilities, manufacturers, insurance companies, stamps, estates, and excises.

By the time the war ended in 1918, the bureau had collected almost $9 billion—more than the combined cost of all the other wars in the nation's history. However, this amount paid only one-quarter of the country's war debt; the government borrowed money to pay for the other three-quarters.

The income tax, a munitions profits tax, and other internal taxes provided most of the revenue during World War I. Even before the war, internal revenue taxes had begun to produce more income than customs duties on imports. But during the war, the income tax was expanded to include more people, and it became one of the government's most important sources of income.

Even so, only about 5 percent of the population made enough money to be required to pay income taxes in 1918. Those who had to pay still opposed it, but the war made it easier for the government to justify the tax and increase the tax rates. To make the tax more acceptable, the Bureau of Internal Revenue organized a large public relations campaign explaining how necessary taxes were to finance the war. Most people began to see their tax payments as a patriotic duty—their contribution to the war effort.

The voluntary system of taxation began during this period. Unlike the Civil War taxpayers, the new taxpayers didn't wait for a bill from the Bureau of Internal Revenue. Instead, when they filled out the income tax forms, they calculated their own taxes and paid the government the amount they "assessed" themselves. Of course, the Bureau of Internal Revenue checked the taxpayers' figures and told them if their calculations were incorrect. Today's voluntary tax system operates the same way.

Prohibition and Depression

When World War I ended, the government reduced its taxes, but the Bureau of Internal Revenue remained active. During the 1920s, the prohibition against selling alcoholic beverages expanded the bureau's role. Prohibition, sometimes called a "noble experiment," began in 1919 with the passage of the Constitution's Eighteenth Amendment and ended in 1933 when the Twenty-first Amendment repealed it. During the intervening years, federal law and the Constitution prohibited the sale of whiskey, wine, beer, and any other beverages that contained more than .5 percent alcohol. (Ordinary beer contains about 4.5 percent alcohol.) The government charged the Bureau of Internal Revenue with the duty of keeping the country dry and appointed a special commissioner of prohibition.

To enforce Prohibition, the Bureau of Internal Revenue often had to destroy confiscated alcohol.

Storing alcohol in a hollow cane flask was one way Americans got around the Prohibition laws.

    The Bureau of Internal Revenue was given these responsibilities because it had been enforcing the federal tax laws on alcohol since 1862, and it knew the industry well. Bureau agents, or revenuers, had earned a reputation for tracking down illegal stills and catching tax evaders. Because of this, many people assumed that revenuers would be the best people to stamp out alcohol altogether.

    However, getting rid of alcohol proved to be much harder than taxing it. A large part of the country refused to obey the new law. Illegal sellers of alcohol sprang up everywhere, sometimes under the control of organized crime. So the Bureau of Internal Revenue had to enforce an unpopular law against mobsters who had the money and weapons to try to circumvent it.

Yet the Bureau of Internal Revenue earned a good reputation for law enforcement during Prohibition. In the 1920s and 1930s, its agents teamed up with members of the Federal Bureau of Investigation and the Justice Department to send some of America's most notorious criminals to jail. However, public opposition to Prohibition remained strong. In 1933, the government repealed the prohibition laws, and the Bureau of Internal Revenue returned to collecting taxes.

Before Prohibition was repealed, the country faced more urgent problems. Since 1929, the world had developed such severe economic problems that people still refer to that era as the Great Depression. Businesses went bankrupt, millions of people couldn't find jobs, banks failed, and people lost all of the money they had saved. The government seemed to be heading for bankruptcy, too. Tax collections fell because people had no money. The government spent far more than it took in.

During the depression, many people blamed businessmen and the rich—often unfairly—for the nation's economic troubles. They began to demand that the government do more about its economic problems. But to do more, the government needed more money. So it raised taxes, especially those affecting the rich. The new income tax rates topped the ones paid during World War I.

Too poor to buy food or pay taxes, many people found meals at soup kitchens during the depression.

The depression not only increased income taxes, but also gave the Bureau of Internal Revenue a new tax to collect. As part of the New Deal plan for economic recovery, President Franklin Roosevelt signed the Social Security Act into law in 1935. The program called for people to pay a tax on their wages into the social security fund while they were working so they could draw money out of it after they retired. The employee would pay half of the tax and the employer would pay the other half. The government charged the Bureau of Internal Revenue with collecting this new tax, too.

World War II

In many ways, World War II helped make the world what it is today. It gave Americans such things as radar, jet planes, electronic calculators, and the atomic bomb. It also produced the income tax system that is currently in use.

After the first world war, Americans swore they would never fight outside of North or South America again. But when war broke out in Europe in 1939, President Roosevelt and many others felt it was just a matter of time before the United States would have to get involved in it. About two years after the war in Europe began, Japanese planes attacked the United States'

Roosevelt signed the Social Security Act, creating a new tax.

fleet at Pearl Harbor, Hawaii. In support of Japan, Hitler's Germany declared war on the United States, and America found itself deeply involved in the war.

The federal government quickly realized that this war was going to require huge amounts of money. Although Congress passed laws that increased several different taxes, the country still needed a tax that raised large amounts of money cheaply and easily. A revised version of the income tax offered just what was needed. The government lowered the amount of taxable income until almost every person with a job was subject to income tax. In 1939 under the old income tax, 6.5 million people paid $1 billion of income tax and 550,000 corporations provided $1.1 billion. By 1945 under the revised income tax, 48 million people paid $19 billion of income tax and 603,000 corporations paid $16 billion of income and excess profits taxes.

To collect income tax from so many people and businesses, the government needed a new system. In 1941, the Treasury Department asked Congress to pass a law letting it use the Civil

Japan's attack on Pearl Harbor pushed America into war.

World War II required M-5 tanks and other expensive equipment and supplies. To finance this war, the government increased taxes, including the income tax.

War method of withholding income tax from wages and other payments. Under this system, the Bureau of Internal Revenue would tell an employer how much to take out of an employee's wages to pay his tax bill from the previous year. The employer would collect the tax and send it to the bureau. Then the bureau would simply check the payments for accuracy.

Before Congress passed this law, however, a banker named Beardsley Ruml (pronounced "Rummel") had a more popular idea. He thought that using this year's income to pay last year's taxes could cause problems. For example, if the army drafted a young man who had been earning a good salary, he wouldn't be able to pay the high taxes on his previous year's salary while earning a much lower salary in the army. Ruml contended that the system would work better if taxes were paid when money was earned. Then the young man in the example could pay taxes on the high salary while he was earning that salary.

43

Ruml revised the withholding tax plan.

The Bureau of Internal Revenue combined Ruml's idea with the old system of withholding tax from wages, and the current method of income tax collection was born. Based on information from employees and Internal Revenue tables, an employer would estimate how much tax an employee owed on each paycheck. Then the employer would deduct, or withhold, the tax from the employee's pay and send it to Internal Revenue. At the end of the year, the employee would settle his account with the bureau by sending in a form, called a return, showing how much tax he owed. If the employer withheld too much tax money, the employee would get a refund; if the employer held out too little, the employee would pay the difference to Internal Revenue.

The new system worked very well. By 1945, income taxes supplied more than half of the government's revenue, and nearly four-fifths of that came from withholding.

The Computer Age

After World War II, the United States didn't return to a completely peaceful time as it had after other wars. Because of the Communist threat, the country continued to have high defense costs and needed taxes to support them. The income tax remained one of the government's main sources of revenue.

This revenue increased steadily as the number of taxpayers and tax returns multiplied.

As the tax system grew, so did the Bureau of Internal Revenue. But in 1952, a series of scandals rocked the bureau: investigators caught Internal Revenue agents accepting bribes and fixing tax cases in court. In response, the Bureau of Internal Revenue dismissed these employees and reorganized its internal management. At the same time, it was renamed the Internal Revenue Service to emphasize the taxpayer service aspect of the agency's responsibilities.

By the early 1960s, the growing number of taxpayers and the increasingly complex tax laws threatened to bury the IRS in paperwork. So the agency began to use computers to process paperwork more efficiently. By the end of the decade, it had a

As the tax system grew after World War II, the Bureau of Internal Revenue turned to computers to improve efficiency.

Scientists testified before a special House committee investigating tax-free foundations.

computer file on everyone in the United States who filed a tax return.

The computer became a powerful tool for tax collection. Income payers, such as employers who paid wages or banks that paid interest, had to report to the IRS those who received payments and the amounts paid. Then the IRS's computers matched these reports with the returns of employees or bank depositors to be sure the amount due was reported correctly. If the amounts differed, IRS agents would investigate the discrepancy.

But the computer age also created new problems for the IRS. By the 1970s, many people had become suspicious of the IRS's power. Some said the agency investigated tax returns for political reasons. Others believed it gave White House aides information about the president's political enemies.

These stories led to changes in the IRS. The president appointed a new commissioner and made him completely independent of pressures from other government agencies. Congress passed new laws protecting the taxpayers' privacy. The IRS itself laid down stricter rules for its employees in dealing with taxpayers and tax information and set up a new office designed to handle taxpayers' complaints.

In the 1980s, the IRS had to face another problem. Computer technology was changing so quickly that the best computer equipment available one year was outdated by the next. With its enormous annual workload, the IRS couldn't afford to change computer systems so frequently. Nor could it risk losing tax information, a problem that's likely to occur during an equipment change. Every taxpayer expected the IRS to be able to find his tax records, if necessary. Losing even a very small fraction of its records could have gotten the IRS into trouble. For instance, if it had lost just .1 percent of the individual tax returns filed in 1984, 96,000 taxpayers would have been angry. They might have even gotten angry enough to write to their congressmen or to attract media attention, which could have led to congressional investigations and political conflicts for the IRS.

Eventually, the IRS's computer equipment became so outdated that it had to be replaced. In 1985, the IRS installed a new computer system for part of its work, which created many problems in finding people's tax records. Because of the transition, many refunds were late and many taxpayers were upset. Despite these difficulties, the IRS handled most of its records accurately and carefully during the transition.

James Baker, secretary of the treasury, oversees the IRS.

FOUR

The IRS Organization

To perform its job properly, the IRS has to interact with many other governmental agencies. Its relationship with the Treasury Department is particularly important. Although it reports to, and is a part of, the Treasury Department, the IRS is basically a self-contained division.

The most significant interaction between the IRS and the Treasury Department is their joint effort at developing tax policies for legislative consideration. In addition, the IRS commissioner is a member of the secretary of the treasury's staff. He takes part in staff meetings regularly and provides an annual report to the secretary. The commissioner's legal officer, the chief counsel, also acts as assistant general counsel to the Treasury Department. Other IRS divisions also provide services to the Treasury Department; for example, the IRS Data Center in Detroit prepares the Treasury Department's payroll.

The IRS also interacts with the Department of Justice. Its tax court, district courts, and claims courts provide indepen-

Washington, D.C., is the home of the IRS headquarters.

dent reviews of disputes between taxpayers and the IRS. Decisions in these courts ensure uniform interpretation of policy.

The IRS coordinates its overseas activities through the State Department. To reach United States citizens who live abroad, the IRS sends tax information and help through embassies and consulates that are maintained by the Department of State.

The IRS works with many other federal organizations, but the most important is Congress. In Congress, permanent tax-writing committees (the House Ways and Means Committee and the Senate Finance Committee) frequently call on the IRS for technical aid and information. Then Congress writes the tax laws, which the IRS must administer and enforce. Congress also has the power to investigate alleged IRS abuses. In addition, the Appropriations Committee of Congress reviews the IRS's annual budget requests. It then allocates funds from the federal budget to run the agency.

The IRS also works with state tax agencies in a tax audit program. They exchange tax return information, often by computer, to be sure taxpayers have filed comparable returns. Frequently, these IRS-state tax audits result in additional revenue.

Because the IRS is a large and complex agency, its structure must enable it to use its resources efficiently. The IRS organization is decentralized and has three levels: the national office headquartered in Washington, D.C.; the seven regional offices; and the district offices, service centers, and data processing centers located around the country. A district office may have one or more local offices, depending on the needs of the IRS and the taxpayers. To help the IRS function most efficiently, some jobs are split between offices.

The National Office

The national office is the headquarters of the IRS. It develops national programs and policies for administering tax laws and directs the activities of the regional offices, district offices, and service centers. The commissioner of internal revenue runs the agency from the national office.

Because the IRS is part of the Treasury Department, the commissioner reports to the secretary of the treasury. However, the commissioner is appointed by the president of the United States. (Usually, a new commissioner takes over whenever a new president is elected.) The commissioner is an important person in the government who advises the secretary of the trea-

Americans living abroad receive tax information through their embassies, such as this one in Guatemala.

sury and, sometimes, the president. In addition, he supervises the 95,000 civil servants who work for the IRS.

The commissioner supervises the deputy commissioner and three associate commissioners who are responsible for operations, policy and management, and data processing. The associate commissioner in charge of the operations division has criminal investigators who check on taxpayers who may be cheating, examiners who review taxpayers' returns and other records, collection officers who collect bills for the IRS, and workers who oversee employee plans and exempt organizations.

Under the direction of an associate commissioner, the policy and management division provides support and services such as facilities management and security to all IRS divisions; performs financial, research, and planning activities for the organization; and handles all human resource functions, such as hiring and training. In short, the policy and management division keeps the organization running. (Each regional office and all other offices have a similar division.)

The third associate commissioner runs the data processing division, which manages all computer services and receives and processes tax returns and other information sent in by taxpayers and businessmen. It checks the returns and gets correct information from taxpayers, if necessary. It also records the information in the computer and counts and deposits the tax money so the Treasury Department can use it to pay the government's bills. In addition, this division works to redesign the tax system.

Ten assistant commissioners function under the associate commissioners and run different parts of the IRS. Usually, the assistant commissioners' titles relate to their specific jobs. The associate commissioner of operations supervises assistant commissioners of criminal investigation, examination, collection, and employee plans and exempt organizations. The associate commissioner of policy and management oversees the assistant

The IRS Organization

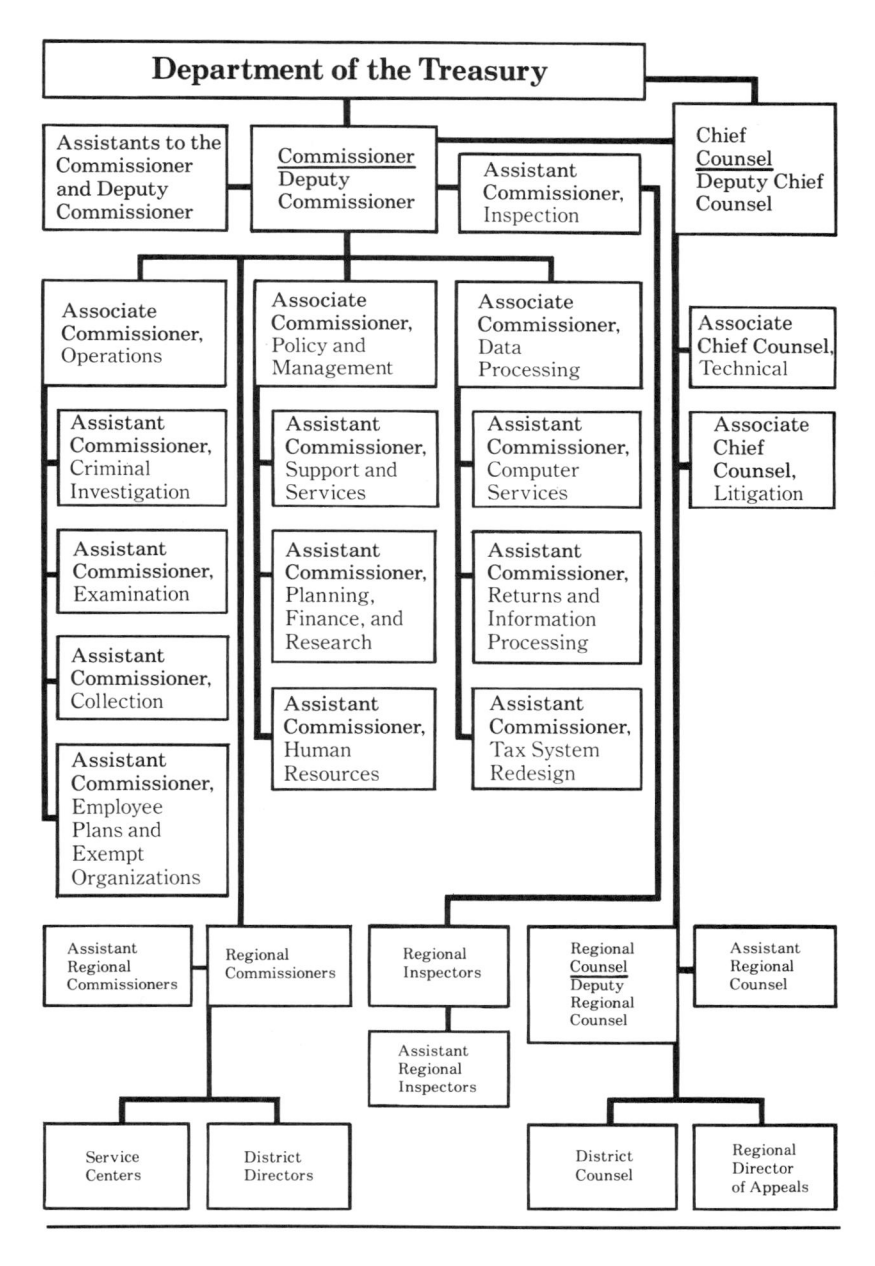

Department of the Treasury

- Assistants to the Commissioner and Deputy Commissioner
- Commissioner / Deputy Commissioner
- Assistant Commissioner, Inspection
- Chief Counsel / Deputy Chief Counsel

- Associate Commissioner, Operations
  - Assistant Commissioner, Criminal Investigation
  - Assistant Commissioner, Examination
  - Assistant Commissioner, Collection
  - Assistant Commissioner, Employee Plans and Exempt Organizations
- Associate Commissioner, Policy and Management
  - Assistant Commissioner, Support and Services
  - Assistant Commissioner, Planning, Finance, and Research
  - Assistant Commissioner, Human Resources
- Associate Commissioner, Data Processing
  - Assistant Commissioner, Computer Services
  - Assistant Commissioner, Returns and Information Processing
  - Assistant Commissioner, Tax System Redesign
- Associate Chief Counsel, Technical
- Associate Chief Counsel, Litigation

- Assistant Regional Commissioners
- Regional Commissioners
- Regional Inspectors
  - Assistant Regional Inspectors
- Regional Counsel / Deputy Regional Counsel
- Assistant Regional Counsel

- Service Centers
- District Directors
- District Counsel
- Regional Director of Appeals

53

commissioners responsible for support and services; planning, finance, and research; and human resources. The associate commissioner of data processing manages the assistant commissioners of computer services, returns and information processing, and tax system redesign.

Reporting directly to the commissioner's office, another assistant commissioner is in charge of inspections at the national and other levels of the agency. Because the IRS collects so much money from so many people, it has to be especially careful that its employees don't take bribes or steal. So the inspection division checks on employees to be sure they're doing their jobs correctly and honestly. It tests to see if they're following the IRS rules and investigates possible crimes by IRS employees. Inspection employees also study the IRS's operating methods to improve their efficiency.

The IRS chief counsel also reports to the commissioner in the national office. He provides legal services to the IRS and acts as assistant general counsel for the Treasury Department. The office of the chief counsel interprets the tax laws, helps prepare court cases involving those laws, and acts as the IRS's lawyer in other ways.

The chief counsel's office interprets tax laws that are part of the United States Code.

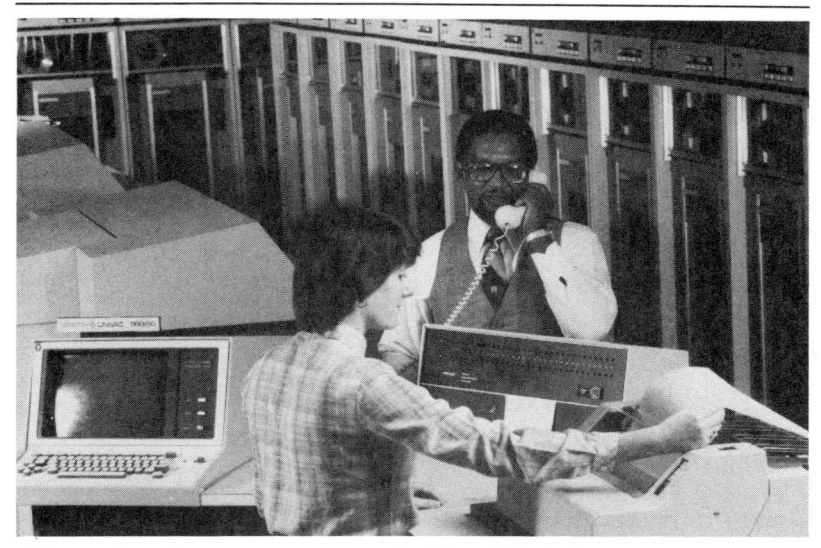

The national computer center in West Virginia reports directly to the IRS national office.

Other positions in the national office include assistants to the commissioner who are responsible for public affairs, equal opportunity, legislative liaisons, and taxpayer advocacy. The national office also controls the national computer center in West Virginia and the data center in Michigan.

Other IRS Offices and Centers

The IRS has seven regional offices to manage and assess the workings of the district offices and service centers. A regional commissioner runs each office and reports to the commissioner of the IRS. Five assistant regional commissioners report to the regional commissioners and have titles similar to their counterparts in the national office. The regional offices also include staff members of the regional counsel (who reports to the chief counsel) and a regional inspector (who reports to the assistant commissioner of inspection in the national office).

Internal Revenue Service
Offices and Service Centers

Western Region

Midwest Region

Southwest Region

Washington
Oregon
Idaho
California
Nevada
San Francisco
Fresno
Hawaii
Alaska
Montana
North Dakota
South Dakota
Wyoming
Nebraska
Ogden
Utah
Colorado
Kansas
Arizona
New Mexico
Oklahoma
Texas
Dallas
Austin

North-Atlantic Region

Maine
New Hampshire
Vermont
New York
Andover
Massachusetts
Rhode Island
Connecticut
New York City

Central Region

nesota
Wisconsin
Michigan
wa
Chicago
Illinois
Indiana
Ohio **Cincinnati**
West Virginia
Kansas City
Missouri
Covington Kentucky

Mid-Atlantic Region

Pennsylvania
Philadelphia
New Jersey
Delaware
Maryland
Virginia
Washington, D.C.

Southeast Region

Tennessee
North Carolina
Arkansas
Memphis
South Carolina
Mississippi
Atlanta
Alabama
Georgia
Louisiana
Florida

LEGEND
▲ National Office
● Regional Offices
■ Service Centers

A district director administers each of the 63 IRS district offices. The district offices handle taxpayer services, collections, examinations, criminal investigations, resource management, and employee plans and exempt organizations. Each director must deposit district taxes and process new and renewal applications for IRS practitioners (attorneys and others who represent taxpayers before the IRS). A district may set up local offices if the taxpayers need them and if the workload demands them.

The IRS has ten service centers located around the country to process tax returns and other information, to assess and cer-

The IRS service center in Andover, Massachusetts, is one of ten centers that process tax returns, handle tax-related information, and track the taxes they collect.

tify tax refunds, and to keep track of all of the taxes it collects. Each service center is managed by the regional commissioner in its area. The centers are located in California, Georgia, Kentucky, Massachusetts, Missouri, New York, Pennsylvania, Tennessee, Texas, and Utah.

Careers with the IRS

Because the IRS is such a large, complex organization, it offers a great variety—and a great number—of career opportunities in many locations around the country as well as in its headquarters in Washington, D.C.

The *internal revenue agent* position is especially suitable for candidates with college degrees in accounting. The typical revenue agent examines and audits the accounting books and records of individuals, partnerships, trusts, and corporations to assess their correct federal tax liabilities.

For the position of *tax auditor*, the IRS will consider applicants who have any type of college degree. However, it prefers those who have taken business-related courses. A tax auditor specializes in answering federal income tax questions on individual and small business returns.

Any college degree can qualify a candidate to be a *revenue officer*, but the IRS prefers to hire those who have studied business-related subjects. Revenue officers are "field" workers who are responsible for collecting unpaid taxes and helping taxpayers understand and meet their tax obligations.

The *special agent* position requires a college degree with at least 12 semester hours of accounting. Job responsibilities include investigation of possible cases of criminal tax fraud and the ability to take enforcement actions against criminal violations.

Internal security inspectors conduct a variety of investigations related to internal IRS operations. Positions are available

The IRS offers career opportunities in many fields, including accounting, law, and data processing.

for applicants with college degrees in any major.

For the position of *internal auditor*, the IRS requires a college degree in accounting. As a member of a professional staff of accountants, an internal auditor plans and conducts management audits of all IRS operations, including data processing.

Located in Washington, D.C., the *tax law specialist* position requires a college degree in accounting or law. Applicants may substitute a college degree in business administration, economics, or finance with 12 semester hours of accounting. A tax law specialist gives official interpretations and guidance to individuals, businesses, and IRS employees on tax questions that have no precedents.

For the position of *attorney (estate tax)*, the IRS requires a law degree and bar membership within 14 months of initial employment. The duties of this professional position include applying laws and regulations to determine federal estate and gift tax liability.

Although many of these positions require a college degree, the IRS has many others that require different backgrounds, such as data processing, secretarial, and personnel. Most of the jobs in the IRS are in civil service, so applicants must complete Form SF-171, the Personal Qualifications Statement. Some positions require applicants to take the Professional and Administrative Career Examination, called PACE. Local IRS offices can provide more information about careers with the agency.

Today, machines handle most of the information that reaches the IRS from more than 100 million taxpayers, and the computer master file stores all of the data.

FIVE

How the IRS Works

The main purpose of the IRS—collecting taxes for the government—is not an easy job. The federal tax system has some special problems. One is that taxes are not popular, but they're necessary. Even though the tax system is voluntary (people assess taxes on themselves), it's not based on contributions; taxes are payments required by law. However, in a democratic country, if most of the people don't want to do something, the government can't force them to do it for very long. So to make the system work, most of the people must want an agency—the IRS—to require them to pay their taxes.

The second problem is that the federal government depends on sophisticated taxes—income, social security, and excise taxes—that require complex calculations. The taxpayers also are fairly sophisticated, and since they already have to do some calculations, they don't mind taking a few extra steps to make sure that they do not pay more taxes than they have to. Some

Experts can show individuals how to pay less tax.

people willingly pay tax experts or buy books on the subject to find out how to pay less taxes. In any case, these taxes require more time and money—for taxpayers and for the IRS—than simpler taxes.

The third problem is one of volume. Social security tax involves almost everyone who has a job, and income tax applies to almost any person or business earning more than a minimum income. These two taxes create millions of taxpayers and tax records that the IRS must keep track of very carefully. Because of this, the agency needs about 95,000 employees to deal with information from more than 100 million taxpayers.

In short, the IRS must collect huge amounts of money from vast numbers of reluctant taxpayers. How does it do this? By relying on the employees who are a part of the IRS system.

The tax system works like this. First, the IRS interprets generalized tax laws by writing rules for the taxpayers. Next, it prepares and sends out forms and instructions so the taxpayers will be able to obey the laws. For those who have additional questions about the tax laws, forms, and instructions, the IRS provides further help through walk-in information centers and programs such as Tele-Tax. Then, as the tax money arrives, the IRS must count it, check on taxpayers to make sure they're paying according to the law, collect from those who don't pay, and settle disputes (in or out of court) with those who believe they owe less money. Because the IRS handles billions of dollars each month, it must monitor its operations and its employees carefully.

Making the Tax Laws

The federal tax system is based on tax laws that are passed by Congress. These laws determine what is taxable and the amount of tax due. Usually, lawyers write the tax laws that Congress passes. But before anyone can act on a new tax law, the IRS lawyers in the chief counsel's office have to interpret it.

To do this, lawyers in the national office read the law itself, study the records of congressional committees and congressmen who discussed the law, and research court decisions that interpreted similar laws. The IRS publishes the lawyers' interpretations, and unless a court rules that the IRS is wrong, all taxpayers must follow them.

Lawyers in the chief counsel's office interpret new tax laws.

Filing the Tax Forms

After the IRS lawyers have interpreted the tax laws passed by Congress, the agency must provide tax forms and instructions for the taxpayers so they can obey the laws. These forms, called returns, are the primary contact between the IRS and the taxpayers. They are also the way most people learn about the tax laws. Every year, most American employees and businesses fill out at least one of these returns. By doing so, they become a part of the tax system.

The purpose of the income tax return is to report taxable income to the IRS. An individual must file a tax return if he earns more than a certain amount of money in a year. In 1985, that amount was a little more than $3,400 for a single person. Because inflation may change that figure, the IRS publishes instructions each year that list the current minimum taxable income. If an employer withheld taxes and an employee earned less than the minimum income, the employee may have to file a return to get a refund. A married couple may file together on one return, called a joint return, and calculate their taxes under different rules than those that apply to a single person.

W-2 forms provide data needed to complete a tax return.

IRS tax returns give taxpayers a place to record income, subtract deductions, and figure the tax due.

Most taxpayers receive W-2 forms from their employers. These forms show how much money the employee earned and how much income tax his employer withheld. Employees receive these forms sometime in January and use them to complete their tax returns for the previous year.

Depending on the complexity of a taxpayer's affairs, he'll file one of three kinds of nonbusiness returns. (Businesses have many other forms to file.) Single wage earners who have little or no additional income can use Form 1040EZ, the simplest return. For a slightly more complex return, single wage earners and married couples can use Form 1040A. Anyone can use Form 1040, the complete return, but people with high incomes, business income, investments, deductions, or other special considerations *must* use this form.

Whether they're part-time employees or presidents of large corporations, all taxpayers report the same kind of information. To complete any tax return, a taxpayer must calculate his taxable income. To do this, the taxpayer records his income and subtracts his deductions. Based on this figure, he finds the tax on this amount in the IRS tax tables. That tax is always a certain percent of the taxable income, but the IRS provides tables to make tax computation easier.

1985 Tax Table—Continued															
If 1040A, line 19, OR 1040EZ, line 7 is—		And you are—				If 1040A, line 19, OR 1040EZ, line 7 is—		And you are—				If 1040A, line 19, OR 1040EZ, line 7 is—		And you are—	
At least	But less than	Single (and 1040EZ filers)	Married filing jointly	Married filing sepa- rately	Head of a house- hold	At least	But less than	Single (and 1040EZ filers)	Married filing jointly	Married filing sepa- rately	Head of a house- hold	At least	But less than	Single (and 1040EZ filers)	Married filing jointly	Married filing sepa- rately	Head of a house- hold
		Your tax is—						Your tax is—						Your tax is—	
23,000						26,000						29,000			
23,000 23,050		3,911	3,039	4,819	3,618	26,000 26,050		4,753	3,712	5,918	4,401	29,000 29,050		5,653	4,462	7,058	5,241
23,050 23,100		3,924	3,050	4,835	3,630	26,050 26,100		4,768	3,724	5,937	4,415	29,050 29,100		5,668	4,474	7,077	5,255
23,100 23,150		3,937	3,061	4,852	3,642	26,100 26,150		4,783	3,737	5,956	4,429	29,100 29,150		5,683	4,487	7,096	5,269
23,150 23,200		3,950	3,072	4,868	3,654	26,150 26,200		4,798	3,749	5,975	4,443	29,150 29,200		5,698	4,499	7,115	5,283
23,200 23,250		3,963	3,083	4,885	3,666	26,200 26,250		4,813	3,762	5,994	4,457	29,200 29,250		5,713	4,512	7,134	5,297
23,250 23,300		3,976	3,094	4,901	3,678	26,250 26,300		4,828	3,774	6,013	4,471	29,250 29,300		5,728	4,524	7,153	5,311
23,300 23,350		3,989	3,105	4,918	3,690	26,300 26,350		4,843	3,787	6,032	4,485	29,300 29,350		5,743	4,537	7,172	5,325
23,350 23,400		4,002	3,116	4,934	3,702	26,350 26,400		4,858	3,799	6,051	4,499	29,350 29,400		5,758	4,549	7,191	5,339
23,400 23,450		4,015	3,127	4,951	3,714	26,400 26,450		4,873	3,812	6,070	4,513	29,400 29,450		5,773	4,562	7,210	5,353
23,450 23,500		4,028	3,138	4,967	3,726	26,450 26,500		4,888	3,824	6,089	4,527	29,450 29,500		5,788	4,574	7,229	5,367
23,500 23,550		4,041	3,149	4,984	3,738	26,500 26,550		4,903	3,837	6,108	4,541	29,500 29,550		5,803	4,587	7,248	5,381
23,550 23,600		4,054	3,160	5,000	3,750	26,550 26,600		4,918	3,849	6,127	4,555	29,550 29,600		5,818	4,599	7,267	5,395
23,600 23,650		4,067	3,171	5,017	3,762	26,600 26,650		4,933	3,862	6,146	4,569	29,600 29,650		5,833	4,612	7,286	5,409
23,650 23,700		4,080	3,182	5,033	3,774	26,650 26,700		4,948	3,874	6,165	4,583	29,650 29,700		5,848	4,624	7,305	5,423
23,700 23,750		4,093	3,193	5,050	3,786	26,700 26,750		4,963	3,887	6,184	4,597	29,700 29,750		5,863	4,637	7,324	5,437
23,750 23,800		4,106	3,204	5,066	3,798	26,750 26,800		4,978	3,899	6,203	4,611	29,750 29,800		5,878	4,649	7,343	5,451
23,800 23,850		4,119	3,215	5,083	3,810	26,800 26,850		4,993	3,912	6,222	4,625	29,800 29,850		5,893	4,662	7,362	5,465
23,850 23,900		4,132	3,226	5,101	3,822	26,850 26,900		5,008	3,924	6,241	4,639	29,850 29,900		5,908	4,674	7,381	5,479
23,900 23,950		4,145	3,237	5,120	3,834	26,900 26,950		5,023	3,937	6,260	4,653	29,900 29,950		5,923	4,687	7,400	5,493
23,950 24,000		4,158	3,248	5,139	3,846	26,950 27,000		5,038	3,949	6,279	4,667	29,950 30,000		5,938	4,699	7,419	5,507

After a taxpayer records his income and subtracts his deductions, he uses IRS tax tables, which make it easy to calculate the amount owed on the taxable income.

Income includes wages as shown on the W-2 form, tips, interest income from sources such as savings accounts and any other payments received during the year. Deductions include a personal exemption, which everyone gets (for example, $1,040 in 1985), and special deductions that the tax laws allow, such as contributions to churches and charities.

After a taxpayer completes the form, he signs it, swearing that everything on it is true, and mails it to the IRS. For most taxpayers, filing a return is the full extent of their contact with the IRS.

Other kinds of taxes require different returns. Wealthy people who make large gifts must fill out gift tax returns. The heirs to valuable estates must prepare estate tax returns. Businesses that sell taxed products, such as gasoline or alcoholic beverages, must fill out excise tax returns. Those that pay wages must also complete returns for social security and unemployment taxes. Businesses also must report payments to individuals or other businesses such as wages or bank account interest.

Rather than complete written tax forms, almost all large companies now report tax return information on magnetic tape, which the IRS can enter directly into a computer. Information in this machine-readable format is more convenient for businesses and the IRS to use than information on paper forms. Companies can report all sorts of tax information in machine-readable form, including the income taxes withheld from employees' pay; social security, unemployment, and excise taxes; and payments on their corporate income taxes.

In 1984, the IRS's master file of taxpayers contained records of more than 150 million individuals and businesses. Because many taxpayers file more than one kind of return, the IRS had to handle over 172.5 million tax returns. It collected almost $680.5 billion in taxes and paid out nearly $86 billion in refunds. It received 668 million reports on income such as interest payments and dividends. Fewer than 100 million of these reports were on paper forms; the rest were in a machine-readable format. The IRS employed 20,000 people just to handle all this information and to run the computers.

Businesses that sell alcoholic beverages must complete excise tax returns.

Helping Taxpayers

Because the IRS relies on voluntary tax payments, it provides free assistance to taxpayers to help them understand the laws and calculate their taxes correctly. But in recent years, tax laws have become more complicated, and the IRS has had to work harder to educate and help taxpayers to ensure accurate payment.

The IRS's forms, instructions, and publications are its most important tools for helping taxpayers understand the taxes they must pay. Instructions for completing forms cover most of the common tax rules. For more complex returns, special IRS publications such as the *Farmer's Tax Guide* and the *Tax Guide for Small Business* explain the rules in detail. On request, the IRS also provides shorter pamphlets on special topics such as home sales, deductions for interest paid, and taxes on scholarships. One publication, Number 910, lists all of the publications and other kinds of help available from the IRS for taxpayers.

IRS booklets, such as the two shown here, explain tax laws.

IRS educational materials also help increase individuals' tax knowledge.

The most popular IRS booklet is entitled *Your Federal Income Tax*. It contains everything a typical taxpayer needs to know about his individual taxes. The booklet is free from any IRS office.

The agency also tries to increase taxpayers' knowledge of taxes by supplying educational materials. It produces a high school course called *Understanding Taxes* that comes complete with a text for students and a teacher's guide. The IRS prepares films and videotapes for schools that explain the tax system, the IRS, and how to fill out tax returns. In addition, the agency will lend films and videotapes to clubs and other groups who want to help their members understand the tax laws.

Similarly, the taxpayer assistance division of the IRS helps taxpayers understand and obey the tax laws. It provides a toll-free telephone number for them to call for answers to their tax questions. Taxpayer assistance also provides walk-in centers where taxpayers can bring their forms and records and get advice on completing their returns. However, the division only provides information. Its employees cannot prepare individual returns.

Tele-Tax answers tax questions with recorded phone messages.

Tele-Tax is another IRS telephone service, providing information through recorded messages that cover more than 150 common tax subjects. Each recording, which must be requested by a code number, explains a particular topic, such as how to report income from tips or how to deduct moving expenses.

If necessary, taxpayers can ask IRS lawyers in the national office to give legal opinions on their particular cases. To do this, a taxpayer must send a letter to the IRS explaining his case and asking for an interpretation of the tax law. An IRS lawyer will then write back telling the taxpayer what is legally permissible. If the taxpayer does as the IRS lawyer says and someone else in the agency questions his actions, the taxpayer can use the lawyer's letter to prove that he was legally advised that what he did was right. This helps reduce the number of disputes between the IRS and taxpayers.

In 1984, the IRS handled 42 million telephone questions, 8 million walk-in center problems, and 3 million Tele-Tax calls. It also provided special help such as translating forms for taxpayers who didn't speak English. In addition, it trained volunteers to provide tax assistance to elderly, disadvantaged, and handicapped people, as well as to members of the armed forces.

Processing Tax Returns

When a taxpayer mails his completed return to the IRS, the form joins 840 million other returns, documents, and records in the processing stream. The agency receives more than 90 million individual income tax returns between January 1 and April 15 each year. During the last 60 days of this period, it gets mailbags full of returns several times a day.

How does the IRS process a return that requires a refund? First, the return travels, along with millions of others, to one of the ten major IRS offices, or service centers. These service centers, which are located in different parts of the country and handle most of the paper and computer records that come to agency, are where the IRS starts the process that should bring the taxpayer his refund check, if he's entitled to one.

Machines do much of the processing. To begin the process, a mail-opening machine opens the envelope. Then an employee numbers the return so that it can be found later. (The numbering is performed manually because employees can do a better job of numbering than machines can.) An employee also looks at the return to make sure it's complete and to code it for the computer. For most returns, an employee also has to input the codes and amounts into the computer system. But if the taxpayer uses

Volunteers help non-English-speaking people complete their tax returns.

Form 1040EZ and fills it out correctly, a machine can read the information directly into the computer.

After the information is in the computer, chances are that only machines will be involved with the return until the postman delivers the refund check. The computer runs the data through a program that checks the addition, subtraction, and tax calculations for accuracy. If the return has no mistakes, the computer puts the information on a magnetic tape that goes to the master file computer for further processing.

If the return contains an arithmetic error, improperly copied figures, or some other mistake such as a missing W-2 form, the computer may send the taxpayer a letter asking for the correct information. However, if the taxpayer simply figured his tax incorrectly, the computer may recompute his refund and send an explanation along with his check. If, as a result of this kind of error, the taxpayer paid too much tax, the IRS refunds it; if the taxpayer paid too little tax, the IRS sends a bill for the tax owed or subtracts it from the refund, if one was due.

In each of the ten service centers, the computers put the corrected return data on magnetic tapes. Then each service center sends its tapes to the national computer center in Martinsburg, West Virginia, which houses the taxpayer master file. The national computer center matches the service center tapes

IRS employees sort envelopes full of tax returns by machine.

Service center employees input tax return information into the computer and store it on tape.

with the records on the master file, which contain such information as taxpayer activities in previous years, other returns the taxpayer may have filed, and changes in name and address. The IRS can also use master file data to compare information from a payer of income, such as a company that pays dividends, with information from the people who received the dividends as income.

If this is the taxpayer's first return, the national computer center creates a new master file record. For all other taxpayers, the center looks for discrepancies between current and previous returns. If the master file shows that a taxpayer owes taxes from another year or from some other kind of return, the computer deducts the unpaid tax from the refund. If the master file shows no problems, the computer creates a tape for a program that writes checks. Then that tape goes to a Treasury Department payment center, where its computer writes a refund check and mails it to the taxpayer.

Tapes go to the national computer center for comparison with the master file.

In this example, the taxpayer received a refund, so the IRS didn't have to handle any money. That's typical. Usually, when a business withholds income, social security, and other taxes, the money doesn't actually go to the IRS. Instead, the business sends these taxes directly to local or federal reserve banks that deposit them in the Treasury Department's bank accounts. The IRS receives only the paper or machine record of the amount of money deposited. Actually, the IRS only handles money when taxpayers send it with their returns or when IRS agents collect it from reluctant taxpayers.

However, the IRS must account for all the money owed according to the tax returns. If a return comes in with a check for tax due, the IRS must deposit it into the government's bank account. In addition, the money actually deposited by taxpayers and businessmen must match the amount they say was deposited. So the computers produce records to match tax collections with taxes owed and to identify those who haven't paid what they owe.

The returns processing system also produces a series of reports about taxpayer information. Information about individual taxpayers is private. Although it's against the law to give tax information about individuals to unauthorized people, information about groups of taxpayers is lawful and useful. So special

IRS employees take information from individual tax returns, group it so that individual taxpayers can't be identified, and publish it in the *Statistics of Income* reports. The IRS has produced these reports on tax return information every year since 1916.

Examining the Returns

Although most taxpayers obey the law voluntarily, some do not. Because more people might disobey the law if they thought they wouldn't get caught, the IRS devotes a large part of its staff to making sure that people obey the tax laws.

One way to enforce the law is to check tax returns and taxpayers' records to see that they're correct. While the IRS can't review every return, it must look at enough of them to make each taxpayer feel that his return might be checked. The section of the IRS that does this is called the examinations division, because it audits—or examines—returns and records.

The IRS publishes general information about tax returns every year.

77

The examiners check tax returns and records to see if taxpayers have listed all of their income, have taken only legal deductions, and have figured their tax correctly. They actually examine only a small percentage of the returns. For example, in 1984 they examined only 1,418,787 income, estate, and gift tax returns—about 1.3 percent of all those filed. Sometimes the examiners find that taxpayers have overpaid their taxes and are entitled to a refund, but usually they find that taxpayers have paid too little. Of the 1984 returns examined, over one million taxpayers owed more tax ($14.3 billion), and about 85,500 taxpayers received refunds ($500 million). The rest had paid the correct amount of taxes.

The IRS selects returns for examination very carefully. Because it can't examine every return and because it likes to get as much tax money as possible from the ones it does examine, it examines large returns more often than small ones. (Because large returns report greater amounts of income, they have a greater potential for extra tax collection.) In fact, the IRS examines the returns of some large corporations every year.

But the agency can't assign all of its examiners to large returns. Lower-income tax returns require attention, too. So the IRS also examines some small returns. A sophisticated computer program chooses most small returns for examination based on IRS studies of errors found on all kinds of returns. These studies are a part of the Taxpayer Compliance Measurement Program, or TCMP. The computer program uses a formula to pick out returns that are likely to have the same kinds of errors.

When a return is part of a TCMP study, it gets the most complete examination possible. A computer selects these returns randomly, and the IRS examines them for accuracy. If a taxpayer's return is subject to this type of examination, he has to verify everything he reports on it.

A return's complexity determines how it is examined. A simple individual return is checked by a returns examiner in an IRS office. He asks the taxpayer to bring or send records to verify the information on the return. For example, if a taxpayer deducts money for a charitable donation, the examiner may ask for a copy of the check or receipt. If the taxpayer can produce this and it matches the amount deducted, the examiner asks no further questions. If the examiner isn't satisfied, the taxpayer may be required to pay more tax.

A highly trained person called a revenue agent examines a more complicated return in the taxpayer's office or in an IRS office. For example, an agent may examine a small business return by checking the business's books. As in the individual examination, if the business can verify the information on its tax return, the agent is satisfied. If not, the business may owe more tax. A very complicated return, such as that of a large corporation, requires a team of revenue agents and tax auditors to examine it. Often these examiners have been trained in the finances of the business they are examining.

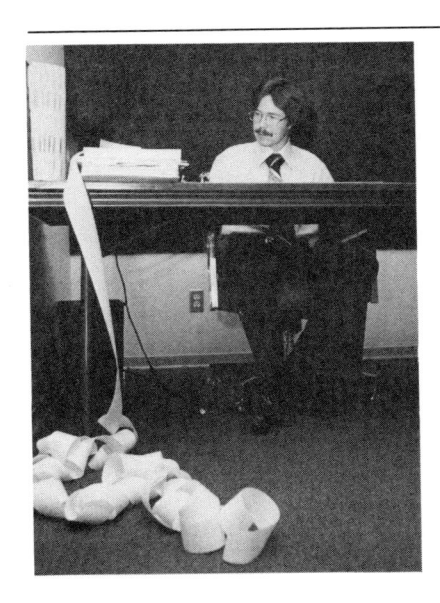

A returns examiner may ask a taxpayer for canceled checks or other records to verify tax return information.

Appealing Examination Results

No matter how complex the examination is, if the taxpayer disagrees with its findings he can demand to see the examiner's supervisor, who will try to resolve the dispute. If the IRS and the taxpayer still disagree, the law requires the IRS to send a formal letter stating the facts in the case and informing the taxpayer of his rights. After the agency sends the letter, the taxpayer has 30 days to appeal. If he doesn't appeal, the IRS can start proceedings to collect the money.

To appeal, the taxpayer must return a notice to the IRS stating that he disagrees with the examiners. Then the agency sets up an appeals conference with the IRS lawyers. The appeals lawyers try to settle disputes out of court, because it takes a great deal of time and money to try a case in court. In 1984, over 75,000 taxpayers appealed IRS decisions to the lawyers, who settled more than 80 percent of the cases out of court.

In many cases, taxpayers convince the appeals lawyers that they are right. If the taxpayer can't get the appeals lawyer to decide in his favor, he can take the case to court and try to convince the judge or jury. If the case goes to court, a different IRS lawyer handles it. Unlike an appeals lawyer who strives to be fair to both sides, the trial lawyer argues only the IRS's side

A team of agents and auditors may review a business's tax return.

Mobster Al Capone was sent to jail for tax evasion in 1932. The tax court handles similar cases today.

of the case and lets the taxpayer's lawyer explain the other side. The court judge or jury decides who is right. For a fee, the taxpayer can try a small case himself in the tax court. However, the taxpayer usually needs time, money, and a lawyer to take the IRS to court.

Investigating Taxpayers

Most disagreements between taxpayers and the IRS are simple mistakes or honest differences of opinion. Tax laws are so complex that it's easy for taxpayers to make such errors as failing to report an item of income or thinking a deduction is allowed when it is not. But in some cases, taxpayers purposely try to cheat the government out of legal taxes.

When the IRS believes a taxpayer has deliberately broken the law or cheated, it calls on its criminal investigators, the special agents of the investigation division. A special agent's job is to gather enough evidence to convict a person of the crime of tax evasion. Typically, special agents combine detective work with accounting. Like detectives, they gather evidence of a crime, but their sources are mainly the account books and financial records that accountants use.

For example, a common way for a person to cheat on taxes is simply not to report all of his income. This happens frequently when income is earned illegally, as in drug dealing. The slick drug dealer runs a cash business and leaves no records of his purchases or sales, so it is hard to prove that he is cheating on his taxes.

However, IRS special agents catch many drug dealers and other tax evaders by using their accounting skills. To convince a jury that a drug dealer had income he didn't pay taxes on, the agent lists all of the cars, boats, clothes, and houses the dealer owns, as well as the expensive restaurants and resorts he has visited, and the suitcases full of cash he had when he was caught. The agent adds up the value of these things and subtracts the income that the dealer reported to the IRS. A difference of hundreds of thousands of dollars will probably convince the jury that the dealer tried to avoid paying taxes.

Collecting from Reluctant Taxpayers

When the IRS is sure that a taxpayer owes money (and the court is sure, too, if the case has gone to court), it may call on its collections division. Collections employees, who are called revenue officers, work like bill collectors to get the government's tax money. They are among the most powerful and feared people in the government.

The collection process begins when a taxpayer receives a notice that he owes taxes. If he pays them, the IRS closes the case. If he protests and says he doesn't owe the money, the examiners and the appeals lawyers discuss it with him. But if the taxpayer doesn't answer at all, or if he refuses to pay after the appeals lawyers and the courts have said he must, the revenue officers start proceedings to get the money.

They begin like regular bill collectors, by sending letters that demand payment and threaten worse action if the taxpayer doesn't pay the amount due. If the letters don't work, they try the telephone. The IRS now uses a computer system for telephone billing, which dials the phone and shows information about the taxpayer's unpaid bill on a screen. The revenue officer can refer to this when talking to the taxpayer.

If the revenue officer can't collect the owed taxes in this way, the IRS lawyers must get a court order commanding the taxpayer to pay. If the taxpayer doesn't pay, the court order allows the IRS to use its special powers to force him to pay. Then, if the taxpayer has a bank account, the officers can order the bank to give the money to the IRS; if the taxpayer has a job, the officers can take his pay directly from his employers; if he owns a business, they can close it down and take his business property. They can also confiscate the taxpayer's personal property, including his car, his boat, and even his house.

The IRS doesn't use these special powers very often, because it doesn't need to. The knowledge that the agency has such powers is enough to make most people pay their taxes. In 1984, the collection process brought in $16 billion: nearly half was collected simply by sending bills. The rest required extra efforts, including letters, phone calls, and the use of special powers.

IRS employees track delinquent tax accounts. The automated collection system (close-up at right) helps them keep pace.

Protests at the local, state, and national levels have prompted the government to review its tax policies.

SIX

The IRS of the Future

Because the United States is a democratic country, the fate of its tax system rests in the hands of its citizens. And because of this, all citizens need to think of ways to solve the tax system's problems and plan for its future.

For the past several years, the country has been trying to change the tax system; the tax reform movement has made more people aware of how tax laws are made and what they mean. One major question concerns the kinds of taxes to use. Should the system tax income or spending? If it were to tax people only when they spent money, it would encourage saving and boost the national economy. But it would also put more of a burden on the poor, who already spend a greater percentage of their money than the rich on necessities.

Another question involves the IRS and tax collections. One tax reform proposal suggests eliminating returns for people with simple taxes who receive their income from wages, interest, and other sources that businesses already report to the IRS.

In California, some protested tax limits that would cause state spending cuts and the loss of community services. Others have voiced similar concerns at the national level.

While many people would be glad not to file a tax return, others feel that if people didn't file their own returns, they would pay too little attention to their taxes and the government could raise them at will.

Other questions remain controversial. How many returns should the IRS audit? (If budget cuts force the agency to audit fewer returns, more incorrect returns may be processed and the agency may lose additional revenue.) How much power should IRS agents have? Can they enforce the law without harassing taxpayers or violating their rights? Should the IRS simply administer the tax laws or should it play a greater role in making the laws?

Taxpayers should also consider how they want the IRS to do its job. For example, in the future people may complete their returns on personal computers and send them by telephone directly to the IRS computers. Before this happens, taxpayers must ask themselves if a fully automated tax system is good or bad. Would it give the IRS too much power?

No matter how taxpayers feel about these questions, a few things are certain. As long as the country has a government, it will need to have taxes and an agency like the IRS to collect them. And as long as America is a democratic country, its people will have to decide what taxes they want and how they want them collected. They must never forget that the IRS is their agent, doing what they have told it to do.

Using personal computers to prepare and send tax returns to the IRS may lead to a completely automated tax system.

GLOSSARY

Commission—A fee paid to a tax collector that is a percentage of the tax money he collects.

Customs duty—An import tax.

Deduction—A special payment that the law lets taxpayers subtract from their incomes.

Excise tax—A tax that is included in the price of certain goods, such as gasoline.

External revenue—Tax money from sources outside of the country, such as import tax receipts.

Head tax—A simple tax where every citizen (head) pays the same amount of money no matter how much money he makes.

Import tax—A tax on foreign goods coming into the country.

Internal revenue—Tax money from sources inside of the country, such as wage tax receipts.

Joint return—A tax return filed by a married couple.

Master file—An IRS file that contains information on all taxpayers.

Sales tax—A tax that is added to the purchase price of goods.

Social security—A program, funded by a wage tax, that provides money when people retire or can no longer work.

Tax return—A form that reports tax information.

Withholding—Money deducted from wages to pay for taxes.

SELECTED REFERENCES

Break, George F., and Pechman, Joseph A. *Federal Tax Reform: The Impossible Dream?* Washington, D.C.: Brookings Institution, 1975.

Chommie, John C. *The Internal Revenue Service.* New York: Praeger Pubs., 1970.

Crockett, Joseph P. *The Federal Tax System of the United States: A Survey of Law and Administration.* Westport, Conn.: Greenwood Press, 1955.

Goode, Richard. *The Individual Income Tax.* rev. ed. Washington, D.C.: The Brookings Institution, 1976.

Internal Revenue Service. Commissioner and Chief Counsel. Office of Public Affairs. *1985 Annual Report.* Washington, D.C.: Internal Revenue Service, 1985.

Prentice-Hall Editorial Staff, ed. *Internal Revenue Code.* Englewood Cliffs, N.J.: Prentice-Hall, Inc., 1984.

Schnepper, Jeff A. *Inside IRS.* Briarcliff Manor, N.Y.: Stein & Day, 1979.

Whitnah, Donald R., ed. *Government Agencies.* Westport, Conn.: Greenwood Press, 1983.

ACKNOWLEDGMENTS

The author and publishers are grateful to these organizations for information and photographs: AP/Wide World Photos, Bettmann Archive, Department of State, Department of the Treasury, FDR Library/Wide World Photos, H & R Block, Internal Revenue Service, Susan Hormuth, Library of Congress, McKeldin Library of the University of Maryland, National Archives and Records Administration, United States Air Force, United States Postal Service, and UPI/Bettmann Newsphotos. Picture research: Imagefinders, Inc., and H. Armstrong Roberts.

The views expressed are those of the author and do not necessarily reflect those of his employer, the Congressional Research Service of the Library of Congress.

INDEX

A
affirmative action 12
American Revolution 21, 29
appeals 80-81
Appropriations Committee
 of Congress 50
Articles of Confederation 29
assessor 32
attorney (estate tax) 60
attorney general 8
audit program 50, 77-79, 80

B
Baker, James 50
Battle of Bull Run 31
Boston Tea Party 21
Boutwell, George S. 33

C
Capone, Al 81
chief counsel 54, 65
Civil Service Commission 10
Civil War 28, 30, 31, 34, 35, 37, 43
Civil War Revenue Act 31
collection districts 32
collections division 82-83
commission 34, 88
Communism 44
computer center 55, 62, 74-75, 76
computerization of IRS 44-47, 83
Confederates 31
Congress 35, 50, 65
congressional representatives 23
Constitution of 1789 29
Curtis, George William 9
Customs Bureau 26-27
Customs duty (see import taxes)

D
Data Center 49, 55
deductions 69, 88
Department of Justice 49-50
Department of State 8, 50
Department of the Treasury 8, 32, 42, 49, 51, 52, 75
 diagram 53
Department of War 8
depression 11, 38-41

E
Eighteenth Amendment 38
examinations division (see audits)
excise taxes 20, 24, 26, 35, 63, 68, 69, 88
external revenue 26, 88

F
Farmer's Tax Guide 70
Federal Bureau of Investigation 40
federalism 7, 8
The Federalist Papers 7
Fort Sumter 30, 31

G
Germany 37, 42
Grant, Ulysses S. 9

H
Hamilton, Alexander 8, 11
headquarters, IRS 48, 51
head tax 24, 26, 88
House Ways and Means
 Committee 50

I
import taxes 24, 26, 88
income tax law 35
internal auditor 60

internal revenue agent 59, 79
internal security inspectors 59
investigations 46, 47

J
Jackson, Andrew 8, 9
Jefferson, Thomas 8, 11, 29
joint return 66, 88
Justice Department (see
    Department of Justice)

K
Kennedy, John F. 13

L
license fees 33
lien 18, 83
Lincoln, Abraham 31, 32, 33

N
National Civil Service Reform
    League 9
national debt 30
national defense 22, 23
national office of IRS 48, 51-55, 57
New Deal 41
"noble experiment" 38
North America 41

O
organization of IRS 56-67
    diagram 56–57
    map 58

P
PACE 61
patronage 9
Pearl Harbor 42
Pendleton Act 10
Pennsylvania 7, 29
Pollack v. Farmer's Loan and Trust Company 35
president 8-11
Prohibition 38-39
property tax 26, 30

R
Reagan, Ronald 12
refund 73-77
regional map of IRS 58
returns (see tax returns)
Revenue Act of 1862 32
revenue officer 59, 82
revenuers 26, 27, 39
Roosevelt, Franklin 41
Ruml, Beardsley 43, 44
Russia 37

S
sales tax 24, 30, 88
Senate Finance Committee 50
separation of powers 8
service centers 56-57, 58, 73-74
Sixteenth Amendment 35
social security 25, 63, 64, 88
Social Security Act 41
South America 41
South Carolina 30
Spanish American War 36
special agent 59
spoils system 9, 10
State Department (see
    Department of State)
Statistics of Income 77
Supreme Court 35

T
taxation without
    representation 23
tax auditor 59
tax evaders 18, 39, 82-83
Tax Guide for Small Businesses 70
tax law 17, 65
tax law specialist 60
Taxpayer Compliance Measurement Program (TCMP) 78
tax reform 66–69, 73–81, 88
tax return 66-69, 73-81, 87, 88
Tele-Tax 65, 72
tobacco and alcohol 25, 27, 31, 35, 38

transportation 22
Treasury Department (see
    Department of the Treasury)
Twenty-first Amendment 38

U
Understanding Taxes 71
United States Code 54
United States Tax Court 81

W
wage tax 25
War Department (see
    Department of War)

War of 1812 30
Washington, D.C. 48, 51
Washington, George 8, 29, 30
Whiskey Rebellion 29, 30
White House 46
withholding 34, 43, 44, 88
World War I 25, 36-37, 38, 40, 43
World War II 11, 41-44

Y
Your Federal Income Tax 71